# CYBER RESILIENCE

## FOR

# ENTREPRENEURS

### HASSLE FREE STEP-BY-STEP FRAMEWORK TO PROTECT SMBs AND STARTUPS

# CYBER RESILIENCE FOR ENTREPRENEURS

## HASSLE FREE STEP-BY-STEP FRAMEWORK TO PROTECT SMBs AND STARTUPS

**MAHESH P. G.**

CISSP®, CCSP®, CGRC™, CISM®, ISMS, CEH™, CAIIB

Worldwide Published by
**Pendown** Press

**PENDOWN PRESS LLP**

An ISO 9001 & ISO 14001 Certified Co.,
**Regd. Office:** 3767A, Kanhaiya Nagar,
Tri Nagar, Delhi-110035
**Ph.:** 8130886000, 9650072927
**E-mail:** info@pendownpress.com
**Branch Office:** 1A/2A, 20, Hari Sadan, Ansari Road,
Daryaganj, New Delhi-110002
**Ph.:** 011-45794768
**Website:** PendownPress.com

**First Edition:** 2024
**Price:** ₹399/-
**ISBN:** 978-93-6338-335-7



*Layout and Cover Designed by* Pendown Graphics Team
*Printed and Bound in India by* Thomson Press India Ltd.

# Disclaimer

This book is intended for informational and reference purposes only. The author does not provide professional advice or services to individual readers. Additionally, the suggestions and recommendations contained herein are not a substitute for a comprehensive diagnostic of the organization's security infrastructure or the assessment of existing gaps and challenges by a qualified cybersecurity advisor or consultant. All matters regarding your security infrastructure require ongoing assessment in consideration of business requirements and applicable regulatory compliance.

Therefore, the author and publisher do not advocate for immediate changes to your current security posture without proper consultation or security assessments. The author and publisher are not liable or responsible for any direct loss or damage allegedly arising from the information or suggestions in this book, or the use of any risk treatments mentioned herein.

The author and publisher assume no liability or responsibility to any person or entity concerning any direct or indirect loss or damage caused or alleged to be caused by the information contained herein, or for errors, omissions, inaccuracies, or any other inconsistencies in these pages, or for any unintentional slights against individuals or organizations.

*For My Wife, Daughters, Father, Mother, In-Laws and Siblings Who Inspire, Motivate, and Light Up My World.*

# CONTENTS

# NOTE TO THE READER

Dear reader,

Have You Been Hacked? (Maybe Not, But It's Worth Checking)

Imagine this: you wake up one morning to find your company's website down. Customer data is gone. Bank accounts are drained. Panic sets in. This isn't a nightmare, it's a harsh reality for businesses unprepared for cyberattacks.

Cyberattacks are a growing threat to businesses of all sizes. The good news? There's a way to fight back.

This book isn't your average dusty cybersecurity manual. It's packed with actionable advice, real-world stories, and a sprinkle of humor (because let's face it, security doesn't have to be boring). Whether you're a seasoned CEO or a tech novice, you'll find valuable insights to fortify your company's defenses.

—•••○•○○•○○•—

Here's what you'll discover:

➤ Why cybersecurity matters more than ever (it's not just about protecting cat videos!)

➤ Simple steps to implement powerful security measures (without a PhD in computer science)

➤ How to build a security-conscious culture within your team (because knowledge is power)

**By the end of this book, you'll be equipped to:**

➤ Identify and manage cyber threats with confidence

➤ Implement practical security solutions that work for your business

➤ Foster a proactive security mindset within your organization

Let's turn the tables on the hackers. Join me on this journey to safeguard your company's future. Because even one successful defense against a cyberattack is a win.

**Mahesh P G**

# Acknowledgment

First and foremost, I offer my gratitude to the Almighty, whose guidance has been my beacon. My parents' love and sacrifice shaped my foundation, instilling values that guide me.

To my wife and daughters, your support fuels my passion for cybersecurity. Thank you for standing by me.

To standards bodies, law enforcement, and regulators, your efforts in cybersecurity are invaluable.

To my mentors, colleagues, and teachers, your guidance has been priceless.

To everyone involved in this book's creation, big or small, your support is cherished.

And to you, the reader, thank you for investing your time. I hope this book empowers you to safeguard your business and contribute to a safer digital world.

With deepest gratitude,

*Mahesh P. G.*

# About the Author

With over 18 years of corporate experience, Mahesh is an award-winning cybersecurity professional, speaker, and author. He has worked for companies like Philips, Tata Elxsi, and Wipro, as well as financial institutions like Canara Bank (eSyndicateBank) and Indian Bank. Currently, he serves as a Principal Consultant in Cybersecurity at Infosys Limited. His expertise spans across Banking, IT, Healthcare, Utilities, Telecom, and more.

He is a gold medallist in B.Tech. Electronics and Communication Engineering and has an MBA in Information Systems. He is also certified in CISSP, CCSP, CISM, CGRC, CEH, ISO 27001, CPFA, CAIIB, CeISB and holds various other technical certifications from Purdue University, Harvard Managed Mentor, IIBF, and IDRBT.

Throughout his career, Mahesh has held various roles such as Cybersecurity Architect, SOC Manager, Vulnerability Management, Infrastructure Security, Risk Assessments, Access Control, Security Monitoring,

Automation, Compliance, Authoring Security Policies, and Standard Operating Procedures. He has also provided corporate training for police departments and corporate employees.

His effective contribution to an organization resulted in the company saving 40% of its costs. He achieved this by optimising security solutions and bringing about a 60%+ improvement in security posture through fine-tuning and best practices. He is experienced in implementing Cybersecurity Frameworks like NIST, RBI Cybersecurity Framework, and ISO 27001 standards.

Above all, Mahesh is a passionate writer, trainer, coach and mentor, committed to training individuals to obtain leading Cybersecurity certifications like CISSP, CCSP, CISM, CGRC, etc. Helping his clients and delivering measurable results in cybersecurity on a continuous basis remains a top priority for him. Mahesh is also author of the International white paper "The Language of Information Security".

# WHY THIS BOOK?

The internet is a double-edged sword for businesses. It opens doors to a global audience, but it also creates vulnerabilities. Cyberattacks are on the rise, and even a small breach can cripple your company. But what if I told you there's a way to build a strong defense without needing a cybersecurity degree?

This book is your key. It's written specifically to be accessible, informative, and (dare I say) entertaining. Here's why you should pick it up:

> **No PhD Required:** I'll break down complex concepts into easy-to-understand language. You don't need a background in tech to grasp the importance of cybersecurity and the steps you can take to address it.

> **Actionable Advice:** Forget theory. This book is packed with practical strategies you can implement right away, regardless of your company's size or budget.

➢ **Real-World Examples:** Learn from the experiences of others. I'll explore real-world cyberattacks and how businesses navigated them, offering valuable insights to help you prepare for potential threats.

➢ **Building a Culture of Security:** Strong cybersecurity goes beyond just firewalls. I'll show you how to empower your team to be vigilant and proactive in protecting your company's data.

➢ **Peace of Mind:** Gain the confidence to face cyber threats head-on. This book equips you with the knowledge and tools to build a robust defense system, keeping your valuable information safe.

This book is your investment in security. It's the knowledge that prevents disaster, the plan that keeps your data safe. Don't wait until it's too late. Take control now. Open this book, and safeguard what you've built.

❖ ❖ ❖ ❖

# My Mission

I've spent years in cybersecurity, dedicated to protecting individuals and businesses both in Government sector and private/multi national companies. While I can't reach and teach everyone in person, this book is my way of sharing my experiences and expertise with as many people as possible. Its pages know no limits—they can travel anywhere, reaching countless individuals and businesses worldwide. My goal is to empower as many people as possible with the knowledge to safeguard their digital assets and operations.

# FOREWORD

Here's the thing- I don't really know much about technology. I mean, I've been in the information, information technology, and information security industries for over 25 years, and I've written books about this stuff... but I don't really have a tight grasp on current tech and how it works and what it does. It's daunting, trying to stay up to date with all the developments and evolution of computers and whatnot. And, I imagine, if you're a small business owner (especially a small business owner outside the world of tech), you're very much in the same place I am.

We're both lucky, you and I. Because Mahesh understands this stuff. And is willing to share his knowledge with us through this book.

Now--will this book make you an expert in technology? In security? Nope. Not at all. And Mahesh declares that even before the book begins. If you need to get your environment secure, GET YOURSELF A TRUSTED CONSULTANT. That can't be said enough, or sufficiently loudly. However, what this book *does,* what Mahesh gives us is a clear roadmap to begin our understanding of the concepts underlying information security. It's the launching point you can use to start studying the concepts you'll need to grasp to properly protect your data and business. And it does a fine job of it, I'd say.

So start here, with this book, and use it as the first step on your path toward understanding. And we can thank Mahesh for holding our hand as we take that first step.

Ben Malisow

Cybersecurity Leader, Trainer, and Writer

*https://www.linkedin.com/in/malisow/*

# ENDORSEMENT

"Cyber Resilience for Entrepreneurs" is an invaluable guide tailored for small and medium-sized businesses (SMBs) and startups aiming to protect their digital assets amidst an ever-evolving cyber threat landscape. This book breaks down complex cybersecurity concepts into easy-to-understand language, enriched with real-life examples and expert insights.

It covers essential topics such as identifying common cyber threats, fostering a culture of security awareness, optimizing cybersecurity processes, using modern technology solutions, protecting sensitive information, and complying with legal and regulatory standards.

With its blend of practical advice, actionable strategies, and real-world case studies, "Cyber Resilience for Entrepreneurs" empowers SMBs and startups to effectively manage cyber risks and establish a strong defence against potential cyber-attacks. This handbook

is your essential roadmap to achieving ongoing success and resilience in today's digital era.

Sangamesh Shivaputrappa

AVP, Head – Managed Security Service & Cyber Defence

Infosys Limited,

*https://www.linkedin.com/in/sangamesh-s/*

❖  ❖  ❖  ❖

# Endorsement

I had the privilege to read the pre-publication copy of this book "Cyber Resilience for Entrepreneurs – A Hassle-Free Step-By-Step Framework to Protect SMBs And Startups," authored by senior industry leader Mahesh P.G.

This book is an essential companion for startups and small & medium businesses (SMBs) to get their cyber security strategy and program right, as they have constraints in terms of funding, resources, tooling, and often have to make do with less.

Written in an easy-to-read manner, the author has focused on key aspects of cyber security program that needs to be in place to protect the IT infrastructure and sensitive data of SMBs and startups. Drawing upon his practical experience gained in his long career, he offers deep insights into program implementation and helpful tips.

What's impressive when you read the pages of this book is the way the author has presented the multiple facets of cyber security program implementation - from technical to regulatory requirements-in an easy-to-understand format with examples and storytelling.

This concise book is a timely publication, helpful at a time when cyber crimes are increasing exponentially and the threat landscape is evolving at a frenetic pace. Startups and SMBs find it increasingly difficult to operate in such a scenario, often targeted by threat actors – individuals & groups - and this book offers practical guidance on cyber security to them.

Wishing Mahesh and this book every success and hoping startups and SMBs will benefit from reading this book.

Dr Ram Kumar G, PhD, CISM, CRISC, CDPSE

Cyber Security & Risk Leader

Global Automotive Major

*www.linkedin.com/in/gramkumar*

❖    ❖    ❖    ❖

# INTRODUCTION

Did you know that 43% of cyberattacks target small businesses? Many underestimate the true cost, thinking it is just about data breaches. But lost productivity, damaged reputations, and hefty fines can cripple even the most promising venture.

In organizations, particularly for SMBs and startups, cybersecurity often finds itself on the back burner. Understandably, the focus tends to be on the business's development and growth areas.

Just like the perfect balance of sweetness in a pudding or the right amount of salt in a curry, cybersecurity adds a crucial layer of reputation, confidence, and trust. It enhances the business' standing with regulators and stakeholders and instils trust and peace of mind among customers.

Let me share a heartbreaking story about a fellow coach, whom I will call Ryan to protect his privacy. Ryan, who hails from Spain, reached out to me after discovering that I work in cybersecurity. He confided in me about a devastating experience: losing $10,000 in a cyber-fraud.

——∘°○-○○°∘——

It all started when Ryan was approached by someone, supposedly from Malaysia, on Telegram. She promised him high profits through cryptocurrency investments. To gain Ryan's trust, she even shared personal photos and stories about their family, and believing in their assurances, Ryan invested $5000. However, as the weeks passed, he saw no return. When he reached out to the lady again, she insisted on further investment of another $5000 to start seeing profits. Desperate for results, Ryan complied. Yet he still received nothing in return.

Finally, realising he had been duped, Ryan demanded his money back. But the fraudsters refused and pressured him to invest even more. Feeling betrayed and deceived, Ryan wanted to get his money back and get help from a cybersecurity expert. I provided him with contacts for legal assistance, but the process was complicated since it involved two different countries.

Months later, when I checked in with Ryan about his startup plans, I was saddened to learn that he had to resort to daily wage work to support himself and his family. The cyber fraud had wiped out his entire savings. This tragic turn of events deeply affected me and influenced my passion to take an active part in building cybersecurity awareness and skills among people and organisations. Consequently, I have created a digital security awareness program and written this book to educate and empower others to protect themselves against cyber threats.

If you are reading this, chances are you have heard countless times about the growing threat landscape and the potential risks that cyberattacks pose to businesses of all sizes. You are not wrong to be concerned—cyber threats are real, and they can wreak havoc on your business if left unchecked.

You are also not alone. As an experienced cybersecurity professional, I have seen countless organisations, including tech startups and family-run cafes, experience the devastating consequences of cyberattacks. The truth is that no industry is immune, and evolving threats make it easy to feel hopelessly behind. I have also seen organisations lose customer trust and incur regulatory penalties due to negligence in the space of cybersecurity. I have spent years helping small to established corporations, including government and private organisations, transform their cybersecurity posture from vulnerable to cyber-proof. I have seen the confidence and peace of mind of stakeholders, along with customer trust, go up a notch just by safeguarding the infrastructure and valuable data.

What I've discovered along the way was eye-opening. A well-planned cybersecurity strategy is not just about protecting your business from external threats; it also entails creating a culture of security within your organisation and empowering your employees to be vigilant and proactive in defending against cyberattacks.

From my years of experience, I bring you exciting news - You do not have to be a cybersecurity expert to protect your business. In this book, I am going to share my hard-earned experience (and a few war stories!) to guide you through building a simple yet powerful cybersecurity strategy.

No complex jargon, no overwhelming technical details. Just straightforward, actionable steps that work for businesses of all sizes, regardless of their tech expertise.

This book contains the lessons and strategies I have implemented to safeguard businesses against evolving threats. You will discover why cybersecurity is so important and how cyberattacks work, along with the aftermath of these attacks. Plus, you will get practical advice on overcoming hurdles and implementing security measures. We will also explore different defence mechanisms and learn about critical security controls to protect their businesses. With bonus chapters on cyber insurance, data protection, and privacy, this book is a complete guide to navigating the digital world safely and securely.

So, if you are ready to take control of your cybersecurity and protect your business from potential threats, then buckle up and join me on this journey. Together, we will navigate the complexities of cybersecurity and ensure that your business is prepared to face whatever challenges come its way.

# CYBERSECURITY AND ITS IMPORTANCE

Let's imagine you run a cool new coffee shop, brewing up the best lattes in town. Things are busy, customers love your vibe, and you are feeling good. But what if someone snuck in, sprinkled salt on your sugar, and messed with your online orders? Ouch! That is similar to what cyberattacks do to businesses—they disrupt things and damage your reputation.

That is where cybersecurity comes in—it is like your friendly neighbourhood barista, on the lookout for trouble. It helps protect your secret recipes (data), your money stash (financial records), and your online presence (websites and apps).

Sure, you might not have the high-tech defences of a giant corporation, but guess what? You've got something even better - Agility! By implementing smart cybersecurity practices, you can become nimble fortresses, adapting quickly to ever-evolving cyber threats.

Cybersecurity is the valiant knight guarding your digital kingdom. It is the complex recipe that ensures the confidentiality of your secret sauce (data), the integrity of your financial records (the sweetness of success), and the availability of your online presence (the oven that keeps your business warm).

Now, let's move on to the formal definition of cybersecurity and its related terms:

According to the National Institute of Standards and Technology (NIST), Cybersecurity is the protection of information and information systems from unauthorised access, use, disclosure, disruption, modification, or destruction to provide confidentiality (only authorised persons get access), integrity (only authorised modifications permitted), and availability (systems and data availability for authorised users).

Another element to consider is privacy, which is the protection of personal data collected by organisations for business purposes. According to General Data Protection Rights (GDPR), data privacy means empowering your users to make their own decisions about who can process their data and for what purpose. Hence, necessary protection mechanisms must be implemented to protect the PII (Personally Identifiable Information) and/ or PHI (Protected Health Information).

In view of the above, it is important to understand the requirement of Cybersecurity and embrace it as a business enabler to support the growth of the organisation.

**Case Study:** Cybersecurity in Action at ABC Financial Services (The name has been kept confidential and altered accordingly to maintain the privacy of our clients).

ABC Financial Services, a reputable financial advisory firm in Bengaluru, was thriving under the leadership of Mr. Sharma. One day, he noticed that clients were complaining about unauthorized transactions and inaccessible accounts. Alarmed, Mr. Sharma contacted me for assistance. We quickly identified and isolated the breach, recovered the compromised data, and implemented robust security measures such as firewalls, encryption, multi-factor authentication and improved the security posture of the organization. We also provided cybersecurity training for him and his team to prevent future incidents. Thanks to these swift actions, ABC Financial Services restored its operations and regained client trust, allowing the firm to continue providing reliable financial services without further disruptions.

❖   ❖   ❖   ❖

# THE CYBER-ATTACK FORMAT - THE CYBER KILL CHAIN

The Cyber Kill Chain, crafted by Lockheed Martin, serves as a critical roadmap for organizations, especially for small and medium-sized businesses (SMBs) and startups, to help them navigate the treacherous waters of cyber threats.

By implementing a method of breaking down the attack process into stages, the Cyber Kill Chain offers organizations a clear picture of their vulnerabilities. You may imagine it as shining a light on the dark corners where cyber attackers lurk. In the cyber-kill-chain format, each move is strategic. From the initial reconnaissance to the final exploitation, each stage presents an opportunity to fortify defences. By understanding the tactics, techniques, and procedures employed by these adversaries, businesses can mount a proactive defence.

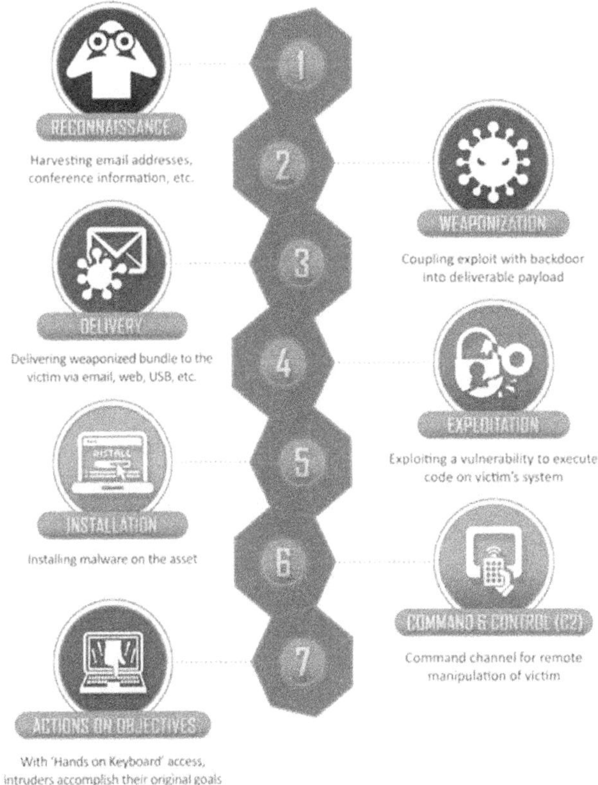


Ref: https://www.lockheedmartin.com/en-us/capabilities/cyber/cyber-kill-chain.html

Let us consider a real-life scenario involving a small e-commerce startup called "TechTrend" which sells electronic gadgets online. Here's how the Cyber Kill Chain phases might unfold for TechTrend:

| Phase 1 – Reconnaissance | The adversaries gather intelligence on the organisation. They scrutinise publicly available information, scan vulnerabilities, and meticulously study the organization's digital footprint.<br>➢ **The process:** Adversaries, posing as potential customers, visit TechTrend's website and social media pages to gather information about the company's infrastructure, software used, employee details, and customer data handling practices. They also search for publicly available information about TechTrend's vendors, partners, and any recent security incidents. |
|---|---|
| Phase 2 – Weaponization | The adversaries progress to the weaponization phase. The malicious payloads—digital weapons like ransomware—are designed to exploit specific vulnerabilities within the organisations. These weapons are poised to unleash chaos once deployed.<br>➢ **The process:** Armed with the information collected during the reconnaissance phase, the adversaries craft a malicious payload, such as a sophisticated ransomware variant tailored to exploit vulnerabilities in TechTrend's outdated e-commerce platform. This ransomware is designed to encrypt customer data and demand payment for its release. |
| Phase 3 – Delivery | By delivering the payload to the organisation's systems through deceptive emails, compromised websites, or other cunning tactics, the digital arsenal is set in motion, breaching the organization's defences.<br>➢ **The process:** The adversaries deploy the ransomware payload by sending deceptive emails containing infected attachments or links to compromised websites frequented by TechTrend's employees. They may also employ social engineering tactics to trick employees into clicking on malicious links or downloading infected files, initiating the delivery phase. |

| Phase 4 – Exploitation | The adversaries exploit the vulnerabilities through lateral movements and unauthorised access.<br>➢ **The process:** Now inside TechTrend's network, the attackers exploit the vulnerabilities they've identified through lateral movements and unauthorised access. They navigate through TechTrend's systems, escalating privileges and seeking out valuable data to exfiltrate or encrypt for ransom. |
|---|---|
| Phase 5 – Installation | Installing the weapon through exploited vulnerabilities.<br>➢ **The process:** Having gained a foothold in TechTrend's network, the attackers proceed to install their malicious payloads through the exploited vulnerabilities in the servers/ systems. When ransomware is deployed, it starts encrypting critical data about the company and its customers, bringing TechTrend's operations to a grinding halt. |
| Phase 6 – Command and Control (C2C) | Establishment of external communication to the attackers' network to remotely control the compromised system<br>➢ **The process:** To maintain control over the compromised systems, the attackers establish external communication channels to their network, known as Command and Control (C2C). This allows them to remotely control TechTrend's compromised systems, execute commands, and exfiltrate sensitive data. |

| Phase 7 – Actions on Objectives | Achievement of the goals by the adversaries.<br>➢ **The process:** Finally, the cybercriminals achieve their objectives. They demand a hefty ransom payment from TechTrend in exchange for decrypting their files and restoring normal operations. Faced with the prospect of significant financial losses and reputational damage, TechTrend is left with little choice but to comply with the attackers' demands, marking the successful culmination of the cyberattack.<br>➢ **NB:** It is never recommended to pay a ransom as there is no guarantee that the attacker can decrypt the data (reverse to the original content). |
| --- | --- |

Ultimately, the Cyber Kill Chain is a strategic blueprint that cybersecurity professionals use to understand, anticipate, and disrupt potential cyber threats.

**XYZ's E-Commerce Under Attack: A Cyber Kill Chain Case Study** (The name has been kept confidential and altered accordingly to maintain the privacy of our clients).

XYZ, a leading online retail company based in Delhi, was enjoying rapid growth with an increasing customer base. One day, they noticed unusual spikes in website traffic and an uptick in customer complaints about unauthorized transactions. Sensing a potential cyber threat, they contacted my cybersecurity firm for a detailed investigation.

—∘○◇○◇○∘—

# The Cyber Kill Chain Analysis

We applied the Cyber Kill Chain framework to dissect and mitigate the attack systematically. Here's how the stages of the Cyber Kill Chain played out:

- ➢ **Reconnaissance:** The attackers performed extensive reconnaissance to gather information about XYZ's E-Commerce Solutions, identifying vulnerable points in their digital infrastructure.

- ➢ **Weaponization:** The cybercriminals created malicious payloads, such as phishing emails with embedded malware, designed to exploit the vulnerabilities they had identified.

- ➢ **Delivery:** These malicious emails were sent to several employees within the organization, attempting to trick them into opening the attachments and executing the malware.

- ➢ **Exploitation:** Once an employee unknowingly opened the attachment, the malware exploited a security flaw in the system, allowing the attackers to gain an initial foothold.

- ➢ **Installation:** The malware installed itself on the compromised systems, creating backdoors for persistent access.

> **Command and Control (C2):** The attackers established a command-and-control channel to remotely manipulate the infected systems and orchestrate further malicious activities.

> **Actions on Objectives:** Finally, the attackers initiated their main objectives—stealing customer data and diverting financial transactions.

## Our Response

By identifying each stage of the Cyber Kill Chain, we took the following actions to neutralize the threat as per NIST Incident Management framework.

> **Detection and Analysis:** We used advanced threat detection tools to identify the breach and map out the attack sequence, pinpointing the entry and spread of the malware.

> **Containment:** We isolated the infected systems to prevent further spread of the malware and blocked the command-and-control communications.

> **Eradication:** The malware was removed from all affected systems, and the security vulnerabilities were patched to prevent re-entry.

> **Recovery:** We restored compromised systems from clean backups and closely monitored them for any signs of residual malware activity.

➢ **Post-Incident Analysis:** We conducted a thorough review to understand the attack vector and improve XYZ's E-Commerce Solutions Cybersecurity defenses cybersecurity defenses. This included implementing stronger email filtering, advanced endpoint protection, and regular employee training on recognizing phishing attempts.

## The Happy Ending: XYZ's E-Commerce Emerges Stronger

Thanks to the structured approach of the Cyber Kill Chain, NIST Incident Management Framework and our swift response, XYZ's E-Commerce Solutions quickly recovered from the cyber-attack. The robust measures put in place not only safeguarded the business from future attacks but also reinforced customer trust. The company continued to thrive, armed with a stronger, more resilient cybersecurity posture.

Lesson - 3

# AFTER EFFECTS OF CYBER TSUNAMI

This chapter aims to share a few real-life attacks that have happened in the industry along with their impacts. This is to provide you with deeper insights into the broader effects that cyber-attacks can cause.

- ➤ **Kaseya VSA Ransomware Attack (July 2021):**

  - **Context:** Amidst a rising wave of sophisticated ransomware attacks targeting critical infrastructure and software supply chains, Kaseya, an IT solutions developer for Managed Service Providers (MSPs) and enterprises, became a high-profile target.

  - **Incident Explanation:** Attackers exploited vulnerabilities in Kaseya's VSA software, distributing ransomware to Kaseya's customers, including many SMBs, via MSPs.

  - **Lessons Learned:** The necessity of rigorous software security assessments and the importance of emergency response capabilities for software vendors. For SMBs, it is critical to manage the risk associated with third-party vendors and service providers through due diligence and insistence on robust security practices.

- **Aftermath:** Kaseya worked closely with cybersecurity firms and law enforcement to address the vulnerability and assist affected customers. The incident prompted a broader industry discussion about the security of supply chains and the responsibilities of software providers.

➢ **Colonial Pipeline Ransomware Attack (May 2021):**

- **Context:** Critical infrastructure sectors became increasingly targeted by ransomware gangs looking to exploit vulnerabilities for significant financial gain.

- **Incident Explanation:** Colonial Pipeline fell victim to a ransomware attack by DarkSide, a hacking group, leading to a temporary shutdown of its operations to contain the spread of the malware. This resulted in widespread fuel shortages.

—∘○○-○○∘—

- **Lessons Learned:** The importance of cybersecurity preparedness in the infrastructure sector and the criticality of having a robust backup and recovery plan. It also highlighted the risks associated with paying ransoms.

- **Aftermath:** Colonial Pipeline reportedly paid a $5 million ransom, and the incident led to increased governmental focus on the cybersecurity of critical infrastructure, including executive orders to enhance national cybersecurity.

➢ **SolarWinds Supply Chain Attack (Discovered in December 2020):**

- **Context:** A sophisticated cyberespionage campaign leveraging a software supply chain vulnerability, reflecting a growing trend in cyberattacks targeting the interconnected systems of global business.

- **Incident Explanation:** Attackers compromised SolarWinds' Orion software update mechanism to distribute a malicious backdoor to thousands of organizations, including government agencies, demonstrating the stealth and scale such attacks can achieve.

- **Lessons Learned:** The critical need for secure software development and update processes, awareness of the risks associated with third-party software, and the importance of detecting and mitigating threats as early as possible.

- **Aftermath:** SolarWinds and affected organizations undertook extensive investigations and remediation efforts. The breach prompted widespread reconsideration of network monitoring, software security practices, and global supply chain vulnerabilities.

➢ **WannaCry Ransomware Attack (May 2017):**

- **Context:** A global cyber pandemic exploits unpatched vulnerabilities in Windows OS, affecting countless systems across sectors, including healthcare, finance, and government.

- **Incident Explanation:** Using the EternalBlue exploit, WannaCry encrypted files on affected systems, demanding ransom payments in Bitcoin. It spread rapidly across networks, causing significant operational disruptions.

- **Lessons Learned:** The necessity of keeping systems updated and patched against known vulnerabilities, the value of having effective, regularly tested backups, and the importance of cybersecurity awareness among all users to prevent malware spread.

- **Aftermath:** The global impact of WannaCry led to an accelerated push for updates and patches for vulnerable systems and a re-evaluation of ransomware response strategies, including the consensus against paying ransoms.

➢ **Equifax Data Breach (July 2017):**

- **Context:** At a time when incidents of data breach are increasing, personal data security has never been more critical. Equifax, one of the largest credit bureaus in the U.S., experienced a massive breach affecting millions.

- **Incident Explanation:** Attackers exploited a known vulnerability in the Apache Struts framework used by Equifax's website, accessing sensitive information of approximately 148 million consumers.

- **Lessons Learned:** The importance of timely application of security patches, ongoing vulnerability management, and the need for comprehensive data protection strategies to safeguard consumer information.

- **Aftermath:** Equifax faced widespread criticism, legal actions, and a significant loss of trust. The breach highlighted the need for stringent regulatory requirements around data protection and the financial and reputational impacts of failing to protect sensitive consumer information.

## ➤ NotPetya Attack (June 2017):

- **Context:** Initially perceived as a ransomware campaign, NotPetya was later identified as a destructive malware attack primarily targeting Ukrainian institutions but inadvertently affecting businesses worldwide.

- **Incident Explanation:** NotPetya exploited vulnerabilities similar to those used by WannaCry, with the addition of using stolen NSA exploit tools. It spread through an update mechanism of a widely used Ukrainian tax preparation software, leading to widespread system crashes and significant data losses for multinational corporations.

- **Lessons Learned:** The critical importance of geopolitical awareness in cybersecurity, the dangers posed by 'wiper' malware disguised as ransomware, and the necessity of secure software update mechanisms. Firms need to adopt a multi-layered security approach that includes robust incident response plans.

- **Aftermath:** NotPetya caused billions of dollars in damages across several global corporations. The incident led to increased investments in cybersecurity infrastructures, more stringent software supply chain reviews, and a greater focus on cyber hygiene to prevent the lateral movement of such malware within corporate networks.

➢ **Uber Data Breach Cover-Up (Revealed in 2017):**

- **Context:** At a time when data breaches were becoming perilously common, Uber's response to its 2016 breach set a notable example of how not to handle such situations, emphasizing the ethical and regulatory implications of breach response.

- **Incident Explanation:** Hackers accessed the personal information of 57 million Uber users and 600,000 drivers. Instead of disclosing the breach, Uber paid the hackers $100,000 to delete the data and keep the breach quiet.

- **Lessons Learned:** The critical importance of transparency and ethical conduct following a data breach. It also highlighted the need for SMBs and startups to have a prepared breach response plan, inclusive of communication strategies that comply with regulations like GDPR and others.

- **Aftermath:** The revelation of the cover-up led to significant legal, reputational, and financial consequences for Uber. It underscored the necessity for robust data protection measures and honest, prompt breach notification procedures, influencing tighter regulations around data breach disclosures.

- ➢ **Dyn DDoS Attack (October 2016):**

  - **Context:** The Dyn DDoS attack highlighted the vulnerabilities within the Internet of Things (IoT) devices and their potential use in large-scale cyberattacks.

  - **Incident Explanation:** A massive Distributed Denial of Service (DDoS) attack targeted Dyn, a major DNS provider, disrupting access to major websites like Twitter, Amazon, and Netflix. The attack was executed through a botnet of IoT devices, including poorly secured cameras and DVRs.

  - **Lessons Learned:** The necessity for secure configurations of IoT devices, the importance of DDoS mitigation strategies in cybersecurity planning, and the potential for large-scale disruptions through attacks on critical internet infrastructure.

- **Aftermath:** The attack led to increased awareness and discussion about IoT security, prompting manufacturers and users to prioritize security settings. It also led businesses to enhance their incident response strategies for DDoS attacks and reevaluate their dependency on single points of failure within their operational infrastructure.

➢ **Marriott International Inc., Data Breach (Discovered in 2018):**

- **Context:** The Marriott International breach, one of the largest in history, illuminated the cybersecurity risks associated with mergers and acquisitions, as well as the long-term persistence of attackers within compromised systems.

- **Incident Explanation:** Hackers accessed the reservation system of Starwood (acquired by Marriott in 2016) and exfiltrated data on up to 500 million guests. The attackers had been inside the system since 2014, two years before Marriott's acquisition.

- **Lessons Learned:** The crucial role of thorough cybersecurity due diligence during the merger and acquisition process. It also emphasised the value of continuous monitoring and detection strategies to uncover and mitigate long-term intrusions.

- **Aftermath:** Marriott faced regulatory scrutiny, legal actions, and significant reputational damage. The breach spurred broader industry recognition of the cybersecurity due diligence necessary in mergers and acquisitions and the need for ongoing vigilance to detect sophisticated, persistent threats.

➤ **Garmin Ransomware Attack (July 2020):**

- **Context:** As ransomware attacks continued to evolve in sophistication and impact, the attack on Garmin highlighted the vulnerability of global technology companies to such threats, affecting their operations and customer services worldwide.

- **Incident Explanation:** Garmin, known for its fitness trackers and GPS technology, experienced a WastedLocker ransomware attack that led to service outages, affecting customer access to Garmin Connect, flyGarmin, and several production lines in Asia.

- **Lessons Learned:** The need for comprehensive cybersecurity in the organisation, including robust incident response plans and regular security assessments.

- **Aftermath:** The Garmin attack underscored the importance of cybersecurity investments and the need for organizations to be prepared for sophisticated ransomware threats.

Understanding attacks like mentioned above and their impacts on organisations will help you plan the right security controls to safeguard your enterprise.

❖   ❖   ❖   ❖

# HURDLES AND IMPLEMENTABLE ADVICE

Meet Alex, the ambitious founder of a promising tech start-up eager to disrupt the industry. Alex knows that the lack of a robust IT security framework will become a bigger challenge for the company. To him, the company's growth fuelled by passion and cutting-edge ideas, will attract attention from both potential investors and cyber threats eager to exploit the chinks in its digital armour.

There is one important point to note from this story -the reason behind Alex's initial oversight is the perceived complexity of implementing an IT security process for a start-up. Alex grapples with the common misconception that security measures are meant only for large corporations with expansive budgets. Unfortunately, this is not usually the case.

Quite often, with tight resources and a focus on rapid growth, security often takes a backseat, leaving the company exposed to cyber risks. Therefore, as the startup gains traction, the absence of a streamlined IT security process becomes increasingly evident. From data breaches to ransomware attacks, the company faces unforeseen challenges that threaten its very existence.

Back to our story Eventually, Alex is forced to confront the harsh reality–the lack of a proactive security strategy has left the business vulnerable, with consequences that could be catastrophic. Alex now realises the importance of having a robust IT security process to avoid setbacks for the business.

Cybersecurity has to be in alignment with business goals and objectives.

Here are the major challenges/mistakes to understand and avoid:

- ➢ **No Streamlined IT Security Process:** In the absence of a well-defined IT security process, enterprises find themselves vulnerable to a myriad of cyber threats, from data breaches to ransomware attacks. The misconception that comprehensive security is a luxury reserved for larger corporations becomes a stumbling block, leaving SMBs and start-ups exposed to potential risks.

  **Implementation Tip:**

  - **Management Support:** Bring in Senior Management buy-in for an IT security process.

- **Comprehensive Security Strategy:** Develop a comprehensive security strategy and an information security policy.

➢ **Remote Working Causes More Security Lapses:** With the rising popularity of remote work, small and medium-sized businesses (SMBs) and startups find themselves at the crossroads of flexibility and security, often grappling with the consequences of insufficient security measures. Unsecured home networks, personal device usage, and lapses in communication security become breeding grounds for potential security breaches. This leads to a critical breach that jeopardises sensitive data and shakes the foundation of the business.

**Implementation Tip:**

- Centralised control of the systems, software and data to be enforced.

- System security, including Endpoint Detection and Response (EDR), Data Leakage prevention (DLP) and VPN/ Proxy to be implemented.

- Mobile device management for BYOD devices to be considered.

➢ **No Budget Allocation for Security Purposes:** Many industries have specific cybersecurity regulations. For small and medium-sized businesses

(SMBs) and startups, the absence of budget allocation for security purposes poses formidable challenges. Constrained by limited financial resources, these businesses navigate a precarious path fraught with potential risks and vulnerabilities. The absence of a budget to ensure compliance can expose SMBs and startups to legal and financial repercussions, potentially damaging their reputation and standing in the market.

**Implementation Tip:**

- Secure management support.

- Update business risks to senior management.

- Highlights benefits like customer confidence and improved reputation.

> **Lack of Skill Sets:** The lack of cybersecurity skill sets poses a significant hurdle. SMBs, often operating with lean teams, struggle to find individuals proficient in threat detection, incident response, and strategic risk management. Retaining talent is also a challenge.

**Implementation Tip:**

- Hire authorised freelancers.

- Appoint qualified consultants and advisors.

> **Security Services are Far Beyond Their Affordable Costs:** For small and medium-sized

businesses (SMBs) and startups, the allure of robust cybersecurity often seems out of reach due to the perception that security services come at an exorbitant cost. These businesses strive for growth and resilience in an increasingly digital world, but the challenge lies in bridging the gap between the necessity for comprehensive security and budgetary constraints.

**Implementation Tip:**

- List down the exact security requirements.

- Explore multiple tools.

- Implement only the required security measures— neither less nor more.

➢ **Lack of Visibility in Cloud Solutions:** Since a third-party cloud service provider (CSP) manages the infrastructure, organisations may have less direct oversight of their applications and data compared to a traditional on-premises setup. Additionally, multi-tenancy, a common cloud computing model where multiple organisations share resources, can introduce potential security risks like data breaches or leaks.

**Implementation Tip:**

- Have controls through tools like CSPM and CASB.

———∘○○-○○∘———

- Ensure the contract is clearer and more aligned with business needs.

- Include clauses for periodic audits and pen testing.

➢ **Lack of Visibility into Data and Storage:** As dependency on cloud solutions increases, including cloud storage, it leads to cross-border transactions and a lack of visibility into critical data stored by the organisation, which often has regulatory requirements for safeguarding.

**Implementation Tip:**

- Clarify data storage locations and legal requirements.

- Build an asset list for the organisation, including data storage.

- Avoid storing critical data on shared drives.

➢ **No Data Protections Solutions Implemented:** The increased use of SaaS solutions and other cloud services requires strict implementation of data protection measures such as classification, the right amount of encryption, and key management.

**Implementation Tip:**

- Implement Data Classification.

- Use Intellectual Rights Management.

- Deploy Data Leakage Prevention Solutions.

- Align with applicable rules and regulations for the organisation.

- Enforce Strict Identity and Access Management for systems and users.

➤ **No Clear Differentiation Between Employees and Service Provider:** Mixing up of staff and service providers often happens, which poses a threat to the organisation due to the lack of security measures on the service provider side.

**Implementation Tip:**

- Create policies for employees, contractors, and service providers.

- Periodical review of roles.

- Implement Multi-Factor Authentication.

- Conduct Periodic Cybersecurity Awareness Training.

- Use non-disclosure agreements (NDA) and penalty clauses.

➤ **No Control Over Third-Party or Supply Chain risks:** Businesses grow by connecting with third parties, which introduces security challenges. Even if an organization has robust security measures, a lack of security from the supply Chain or third party can negatively affect the organisation.

**Implementation Tip:**

- Review the supply chain or third-party security posture.

- Request their latest cybersecurity audit report (e.g., SOC 2 Reports).

- Sign strong non-disclosure agreements.

➢ **Lack of Employee and Customer Awareness in Security:** Due to the agile nature of work and the pressure of delivering the products/services in a very short time, security often gets sidelined, which causes vulnerabilities in the systems. Lack of security awareness among customers can lead to social engineering attacks and unnecessary financial refunds/burdens for the organisation.

**Implementation Tip:**

- Provide periodic security training.

- Conduct simulated exercises.

- Reward employees for cybersecurity implementation and reporting.

- Encourage them to report malicious activities.

➢ **Lack of Security Governance and Compliance Alignment:** Most organisations are dealing with data from external parties, which may have compliance requirements in their country like GDPR to protect Personally Identifiable Information (PII). Hence, it demands the right security governance and compliance alignment to safeguard critical data.

**Implementation Tip:**

- Implement basic security governance, including cybersecurity policies and procedures.

- List down the compliance requirements and global regulation applicability.

- Assign a team to follow these as part of their job.

- Follow standards like COBIT, NIST Cybersecurity Framework, and ISO 27001.

➤ **Lack of Security Audits and Vulnerability Assessments:** Lack of monitoring in the security aspects of the IT infrastructure can lead to vulnerability exposures and exploitation of the threats, causing more devastating damage that even cannot be recovered in certain cases.

**Implementation Tip:**

- Conduct mandatory security audits and vulnerability assessments for critical systems and assets at least quarterly.

- Conduct vulnerability assessments for non-critical assets at least every 6 months.

- Inform top management of the outcomes, challenges, risks, and benefits of addressing gaps. It also helps to get suitable budgets.

> **Delayed Patching of The Systems:** One of the major challenges organisations faces is proper patching of the system on a timely basis.

**Implementation Tip:**

- Regularly monitor system patch releases by OS and application vendors.

- Implement patching as soon as possible after due testing.

- Ensure patching is done for Network and Security devices, including Cloud Assets.

> **Lack of Understanding of Security Technologies:** Due to the plethora of technologies available in cybersecurity, it is challenging for organisations to adopt and implement the right technology according to their business needs. Some clients have implemented multiple technologies but they still got breached on certain occasions. It is important to have an efficient implementation of the solutions rather than adding more.

**Implementation Tip:**

- Have focused discussions with service providers about available security options

- Subscribe to technology newsletters.

- Use threat intelligence feeds to protect against evolving threats.

➤ **The Painful Process in Security Implementation:** SMBs and start-ups are primarily focused on technology and providing services for growth. Implementing security solutions as part of the business is often perceived as a painful process.

**Implementation Tip:**

- Have the right team members or service providers for the security function.

- Educate the IT team on security topics.

- Align with vendors on the security status of their products.

- Follow a framework and have an advisor on board.

➤ **Scepticism Towards the Effectiveness and Reliability of Cybersecurity Solutions:** The lack of skill sets and the evolving threat landscape cause doubt towards security solutions.

**Implementation Tip:**

- Have strong password controls and rotations.

- Follow a security framework.

- Implement best practices and advisories.

- Evaluate through security audits.

➤ **Blind Adoption of Artificial Intelligence/ Machine Learning (AI/ML) Technologies:** This can bring challenges like ML poisoning, causing deviations from intended actions. AI can also provide misinformation and malformed information, which can cause major damage to the purpose for which it is used.

**Implementation Tip:**

- Supervision the AI.

- Adopt due diligence when choosing AI for applications.

- Use AI technologies from trusted sources only.

- Have third party risk management program on AI solutions

Understanding these challenges and implementing the appropriate measures using the given tips promises to enhance the cybersecurity posture of your enterprise.

Lesson - 5

# THE CYBER DEFENCE MECHANISM

Just like thieves, hackers and malware lurk around in the digital industry. Their aim? To steal valuable information, disrupt activities, and damage hard-earned reputations.

Therefore, just as you take measures to protect your physical shop from break-ins, SMBs and startups must take steps to safeguard their digital assets from cyber-attacks. The NIST Cybersecurity Framework 2.0 serves as a guide in this endeavour. The framework offers a roadmap for building a robust cyber defence that can withstand the threats of the digital age.

The Reserve Bank of India (RBI), the nation's central bank, recognised the critical need for enhanced cybersecurity within the financial sector. In June 2016, they introduced the Cybersecurity Framework, a comprehensive set of over 114 controls for all scheduled commercial banks to implement. Having had the privilege of implementing this framework firsthand at the bank I worked for, I witnessed both the challenges and rewards of this crucial undertaking.

The design and implementation process were not without their hurdles. However, the payoff was substantial. By diligently implementing the majority of controls, the bank's security posture underwent a dramatic transformation. Major vulnerabilities and weaknesses in our systems were identified and addressed, significantly strengthening the bank's overall security. This experience demonstrated the immense value that implementing a cybersecurity framework can bring to any organisation.

## The NIST Cybersecurity Framework

> The NIST Cybersecurity Framework (CSF) is like a trusted blueprint for SMBs and startups to strengthen their cybersecurity stance. By customising the CSF's guidelines to fit your unique needs, budget, and risk level, you can create a solid security strategy that shields your important data and systems.

Following the NIST CSF provides you with a roadmap to handle cyber threats effectively. It helps you pinpoint vulnerabilities, set up protective measures, spot potential breaches, react promptly, and bounce back from attacks. This proactive approach ensures your digital space stays safe, paving the way for your business to thrive and expand.

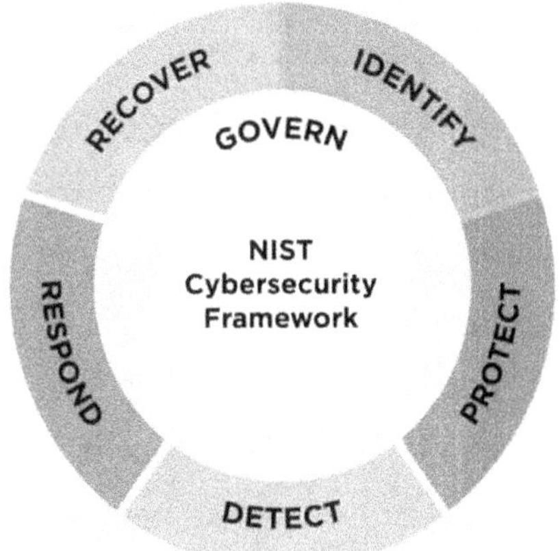


> **Govern:** It acts as a command centre for the cybersecurity functions of the organisation. This function provides outcomes to inform what an organisation may do to achieve and prioritise the outcomes of the other five functions in the context of its mission and stakeholder expectations. It is responsible for establishing a cybersecurity policy, creating a risk management strategy, assigning leadership and ownership, and ensuring ongoing communication and awareness.

> **Identify:** Imagine you are building a castle to protect your kingdom. Before you start construction, you need to identify and understand the threats you are up against. Similarly, in the cyber world, identify the potential risks to your business, from hackers trying to steal your data to viruses infecting your systems.

—∘○○-○○∘—

This means identifying what needs protection, such as customer data, intellectual property rights, employee data, and legal requirements.

> ➤ **Protect:** Once you know your enemies, it is time to fortify your defences. Just like building sturdy walls and gates around your castle, protect your digital kingdom by installing firewalls, antivirus software, access controls, and encryption tools (details on this in the later chapters). This makes it harder for attackers to breach your defences and infiltrate your systems. Consider deploying security mechanisms in both perimeter and internal networks, establishing the right policies, and providing cybersecurity awareness to employees and customers.

> ➤ **Detect:** Despite your best efforts, the enemy may still try to sneak past your defences. This is why it is crucial to set up watchtowers and patrols to detect any suspicious activity. In the cyber industry, use intrusion detection systems and security monitoring tools to keep an eye out for any signs of unauthorised access or unusual behaviour on your network. This involves monitoring network traffic, identifying user and system access violations, and observing third-party behaviours.

——◦○O-O○◦——

➢ **Respond:** If the enemy does manage to breach your defences, you need to act quickly. Just like calling in the cavalry when your castle is under attack, respond promptly to any cyber incidents. Activate your incident response plan to contain the threat and mitigate the damage to your systems and data. For instance, you may need to follow an incident response plan to take immediate steps during an incident and to reduce its impact on the organisation.

➢ **Recover:** Once the battle is over, it is time to pick up the pieces and rebuild. Just like repairing the damage to your castle after an attack, recover from any cyber incidents by restoring your systems from backups, patching vulnerabilities, and strengthening your defences to prevent future attacks. This step includes having the right set of backups to restore after an incident, addressing gaps if any to avoid similar incidents in the future, and auditing/reviewing your infrastructure.

While all these elements are essential, the NIST CSF is a flexible framework that you can adjust to your specific needs and resources.

## Case Study

Implementing the NIST Cybersecurity Framework at ABC's Consulting Services (The name has been kept confidential and altered accordingly to maintain the privacy of our clients).

ABC's Consulting Services, a well-known advisory firm in Gurugram, faced a major scare when they detected unusual activities in their network, raising fears of a data breach. They contacted us, and we quickly implemented the NIST Cybersecurity Framework. We identified key assets, protected sensitive data with strong access controls, set up continuous monitoring to detect threats, developed a robust incident response plan, and ensured a quick recovery strategy. Thanks to these measures, the company was able to safeguard its client information, prevent any major incidents, and continue its operations smoothly, earning even greater trust from their clients.

Lesson - 6

# CORRECT THE EQUATION

One of the most common types of cyber-attacks, such as phishing emails, often reveals a surprising statistic: around 30% of individuals will inadvertently click on malicious links or download harmful content from these emails. This unfortunate reality has led to data breaches and ransomware attacks within organisations. To bridge this vulnerability, it is important to foster a security mindset among employees to effectively counter such psychologically targeted attacks.

In this chapter, we are going to take a closer look at how we can make cybersecurity implementation simpler and more approachable. We will explore the everyday aspects of our organizations—our people, our processes, our technology, and our data—and see how they fit into the cybersecurity puzzle. By understanding and humanising these elements, we can find practical ways to strengthen our defences against cyber threats.

| Area | Business Requirements | Gaps | Addressing the Gaps |
|---|---|---|---|
| People | Cultivate a culture of security awareness and responsibility among employees | ➤ Lack of awareness and understanding of cybersecurity best practices among employees<br>➤ Resistance to change and nonchalant attitudes towards security<br>➤ Internal threats by employees can cause massive damage | ➤ Implement cybersecurity training and awareness programmes<br>➤ Encourage active participation and engagement through incentives and recognition<br>➤ Establish clear reporting procedures and anonymous reporting options<br>➤ Enforce password complexity policies and multi-factor authentication<br>➤ Regularly communicate policies and procedures, conduct compliance audits |
| Process | Create, streamline and optimise cybersecurity processes | ➤ Lack of policy, procedures, standards and guidelines<br>➤ Lack of incident response processes | ➤ Develop comprehensive cybersecurity policies, standards and procedures<br>➤ Develop and implement updated incident response plans with clear roles and responsibilities |

| Technology | Modernise technology stack, invest in cutting-edge solutions | ➢ Outdated systems and legacy applications<br>➢ Fragmented security tools that fail to integrate seamlessly | ➢ Regularly update and maintain security software and implement next-generation solutions<br>➢ Consolidate security tools and invest in an integrated solution |
|---|---|---|---|
| Data | Ensure the security and privacy of sensitive data | ➢ Insufficient data encryption and protection measures<br>➢ Lack of data classification, all data treated equally<br>➢ Vulnerabilities in data storage and transmission mechanisms<br>➢ Excessive data collection, unnecessary data retention | ➢ Implement robust encryption protocols and access controls to safeguard sensitive data<br>➢ Develop and implement data classification and handling policies to categorise and protect data accordingly<br>➢ Implement data minimization principles, define data retention policies |

People, Processes, and Technology are not independent entities, but rather the interconnected pillars of a robust cyber defence. Addressing the gaps in each area requires a holistic approach, where security awareness training empowers employees, streamlined processes facilitate swift response, and cutting-edge

technology shields valuable data. Remember, the most sophisticated security solution is only as effective as the weakest link.

# 13 CRITICAL SECURITY CONTROLS TO SAFEGUARD YOUR BUSINESS

See your business' data as a vault filled with your innovative ideas, vital customer details, and financial records. Like any valuable item, it should be well-protected. Consider implementing security controls by building layers of fortifications around this vault. These measures act as your vigilant guardians, allowing only trusted individuals through the gates while repelling unauthorised intruders. Imagine access controls as sturdy locks, firewalls as diligent security guards, encryption as an intricate combination lock, and intrusion detection systems as sharp-eyed sentinels. Together, these defences form a formidable barrier, preventing any would-be attackers and ensuring your precious data remains safe and sound.

Take a look at some of the measures:

1.  **Security Governance:**

    Security governance refers to the establishment of a framework that outlines the policies, procedures, and responsibilities for managing and safeguarding information assets within an organisation. It involves strategic planning, risk management, and the alignment of security initiatives with business objectives.

    A well-defined security governance framework provides a structured approach to managing cybersecurity, ensuring that security measures align with the organisation's goals and are consistently enforced.

2.  **Application Whitelisting:**

    Application whitelisting is a security practice that allows only approved and authorised applications to execute on a system. It involves creating a list (whitelist) of permitted applications and preventing the execution of any not on the list.

    By limiting the software that can run on a system, application whitelisting helps prevent the execution of malicious or unauthorised applications, enhancing overall system security.

3. **System and Application Hardening:**

   System and application hardening involves configuring systems and software securely to reduce vulnerabilities. This includes disabling unnecessary services, limiting user privileges, and implementing security best practices.

   Hardening systems and applications strengthen their security posture by minimising potential attack vectors and reducing the surface area available for exploitation by malicious actors.

4. **Regular Patching:**

   Regular patching involves applying updates and security patches to software, operating systems, and applications. This practice addresses known vulnerabilities and enhances the overall security of the IT infrastructure.

   Timely patching is critical to closing security gaps and protecting systems from exploits that target known vulnerabilities. It is a proactive measure to stay ahead of potential cyber threats.

5. **Privilege Identity Management (Administrative Privileges)/Need to Know Controls:**

   Privilege Identity Management (PIM) involves managing and controlling user access rights, particularly administrative privileges. The principle of least privilege is applied, ensuring that users have only the minimum level of access required for their roles.

Restricting access to the minimum necessary level helps minimise the impact of potential security incidents, preventing unauthorised users from compromising sensitive data or systems.

6. **Multi-Factor Authentication:**

   Multi-factor authentication (MFA) requires users to provide multiple forms of identification before accessing systems or data. This typically involves something the user knows (password), something the user has (security token), and/or something the user is/are (biometric information).

   MFA adds an extra layer of security beyond traditional passwords, significantly reducing the risk of unauthorised access, even if login credentials are compromised.

7. **Data Protection Including Network And Endpoint Security Solutions:**

   Data protection involves implementing measures to secure data throughout its lifecycle. This includes encryption for data in transit and at rest, as well as deploying network and endpoint security solutions to safeguard against unauthorised access and malware.

Protecting data is essential to maintaining confidentiality and integrity. Network and endpoint security solutions add layers of defence against cyber threats attempting to compromise data.

8. **Cyber Incident Response, Disaster Recovery and Business Continuity:**

Cyber incident response involves having a well-defined plan and procedures to follow in the event of a security incident. Business continuity planning focuses on maintaining essential operations during and after disruptions, minimising downtime.

A well-prepared incident response plan helps organisations respond effectively to security incidents, while business continuity planning ensures that critical business functions can continue in the face of disruptions. It also helps organisations avoid penalties imposed by regulators.

9. **Backups and Testing of Data:**

Regularly backing up critical data and testing the restoration process involves creating duplicate copies of data and verifying that they can be successfully restored. This ensures data availability in case of data loss or a cybersecurity incident.

Backups are a crucial aspect of data resilience, providing a means to recover from accidental deletions, hardware failures, or ransomware attacks.

## 10. Third-Party/Supplier Risk Assessments:

Third-party or supplier risk assessments involve evaluating the cybersecurity practices of external vendors or partners. This includes assessing their security measures to ensure they align with the organisation's standards.

Assessing third-party risks is essential to preventing potential vulnerabilities introduced through external relationships. It helps ensure that external partners follow security best practices.

## 11. Cyber Awareness for Employees and Customers:

Cyber awareness involves educating employees and customers about cybersecurity threats, best practices, and the role they play in maintaining a secure environment. This includes training programmes, awareness campaigns, and the communication of security policies.

Cyber awareness is critical to creating a security-conscious culture. Informed employees and customers are more likely to recognise and avoid potential threats, reducing the risk of security incidents.

## 12. Periodical Audits/Vulnerability and Gap Assessments:

Periodical audits, vulnerability assessments, and gap analyses involve regularly evaluating the organisation's security posture. This includes identifying weaknesses, vulnerabilities, and gaps in the security infrastructure.

Regular assessments help organisations stay proactive in addressing security vulnerabilities and adapting to evolving cyber threats. It allows for continuous improvement and enhances overall cybersecurity resilience.

13. **Email Security Solutions:**

Implement advanced phishing protection measures to identify and block phishing attempts. This includes email filtering, link analysis, and content inspection to detect and mitigate phishing threats.

Utilise malware scanning tools and attachment filtering to automatically scan email attachments for malicious content. This helps prevent the spread of malware through email channels. Implement authentication mechanisms, such as domain-based Message Authentication, Reporting, and Conformance (DMARC), to prevent email spoofing and unauthorised access, reducing the risk of Business Email Compromise (BEC) attacks. The use of email encryption protects sensitive content.

Adopting these detailed security measures including right **configuration and change management processes,** will enable SMBs and startups to

strengthen their cybersecurity defences, mitigate risks, and build a resilient foundation for their digital operations.

It is worthy to note that in the absence of the right skill set, enterprises can approach Managed Security Service Providers (MSSPs) or vendors for the right cybersecurity services. Please ensure that the minimum level of security (Baseline) has been followed in the enterprise.

❖    ❖    ❖    ❖

# GLOBAL FRAMEWORKS TO IMPLEMENT

## Why Frameworks?

Frameworks are like the blueprints for building robust cybersecurity defences. They provide a structured approach, outlining best practices and essential steps to safeguard your digital assets. They are not one-size-fits-all solutions, but rather adaptable tools that can be customised to your specific needs and resources

For SMBs and startups, limited resources can leave them exposed to even greater risks. However, implementing a cybersecurity framework offers a roadmap to navigate these threats. It entails having a structured plan to identify, protect against, detect, respond to, and recover from cyber dangers. By following these frameworks, SMBs and startups can ensure they cover all the essential security bases, minimising risks and protecting their valuable business assets.

> **Frameworks offer several key benefits:**

- **Guidance and Structure:** They provide a clear roadmap, ensuring you do not miss crucial security measures.

- **Reduced Risk:** By following established best practices, you minimise your exposure to common cyber threats.

- **Prioritisation:** Frameworks help you identify the most critical areas to focus on based on your risk profile.

- **Compliance and Trust:** Some frameworks hold industry-recognised certifications, demonstrating your commitment to security and gaining customer trust.

> **Popular Recommended Frameworks for SMBs and Startups:**

- **NIST Cybersecurity Framework (CSF):** The NIST Cybersecurity Framework (CSF) is a voluntary, consensus-based framework that provides organisations with a set of guidelines and best practices for managing cybersecurity risks.The CSF is organised into six functions: Govern, Identify, Protect, Detect, Respond, and Recover. Each function includes a set of subcategories and activities that can be tailored to the specific needs of an organisation.

- **CIS Controls:** The CIS Controls are a set of prioritised, platform-agnostic cybersecurity controls that define a best practice approach to cyber defence.The controls are grouped into 20 critical security controls and 7 additional controls.The CIS controls are designed to be implemented in layers, with the most critical controls being implemented first.

- **SOC 2:** SOC 2 is a type of Service Organisation Control (SOC) report that focuses on the security of a service organisation's systems and processes. SOC 2 reports are based on the AICPA's Trust Services Principles and Criteria for Security, Availability, Processing Integrity, Confidentiality, and Privacy.SOC 2 reports can be helpful for organisations that need to demonstrate their commitment to cybersecurity to their customers.

- **ISO 27001:** ISO 27001 is an international standard that specifies the requirements for an information security management system (ISMS). An ISMS is a systematic approach to managing an organisation's information security risks. ISO 27001 certification can help organisations improve their cybersecurity posture and demonstrate their commitment to information security to their stakeholders.

- **Cyber Essential:** Cyber Essentials is a UK government-backed scheme that helps organisations protect themselves from common cyber threats.Cyber Essentials has two levels: Cyber Essentials and Cyber Essentials Plus. Cyber Essentials is a self-assessment, while Cyber Essentials Plus requires an independent audit.

➢ **How to Choose the Right Framework:**

Selecting the most suitable framework depends on your specific needs, industry, budget, and risk tolerance. Consider factors like data sensitivity, regulatory requirements, and available resources. Don't hesitate to consult with cybersecurity professionals for guidance.

It is important to note that implementing a cybersecurity framework is not a one-time event. Organisations need to continuously monitor and update their cybersecurity posture to keep up with the evolving threat landscape.

# BONUS #1 CYBER INSURANCE – SAFEGUARDING YOUR FINANCES AMID CYBER CRISIS

In the digital industry, irrespective of how vigilant you are, breaches are a persistent reality, and their aftermath can resonate across financial, operational, and reputational realms. However, the good thing is that cyber insurance exists. It provides the support and resources needed to bounce back from adversity. Cyber insurance is the shield you never knew you needed until you did.

## Advantages

- **Financial Safeguard:** Cyber insurance serves as a financial bulwark, alleviating the economic strain of cyber incidents by covering expenses ranging from legal fees to recovery costs.

———∘o○-○o∘———

> **Operational Continuity:** With coverage for operational disruptions, cyber insurance facilitates a rapid recovery, ensuring your organisation's ability to maintain business continuity.

> **Reputation Safeguard:** Beyond financial implications, cyber insurance plays a pivotal role in managing reputational fallout and aiding in communication strategies and swift recovery efforts.

> **Tailored Protection:** Cyber insurance can be customised to address the specific risks and vulnerabilities unique to your organisation's cyber landscape.

> **Incident Response Expertise:** Many policies offer access to expert incident response teams, ensuring a swift and coordinated reaction in the aftermath of a breach.

> **Legal Support:** Cyber insurance often includes provisions for legal assistance, guiding your organisation through the intricate complexities of post-incident legalities.

## What it Covers

> **Data Breach Costs:** Covers costs associated with data breaches, including notification expenses and credit monitoring for affected individuals.

- ➤ **Business Interruption:** Addresses financial losses resulting from operational disruptions caused by cyber incidents.

- ➤ **Ransomware Payments:** Covers ransom payments in the event of a ransomware attack, mitigating financial losses.

- ➤ **Liability Costs:** Liability costs refer to the financial responsibilities and obligations that an individual or entity may incur because of legal claims or lawsuits.

- ➤ **Reputation Management:** Covers costs associated with public relations and crisis communications to mitigate reputational damage.

## Challenges and Complications

- ➤ **Policy Specificity:** Ensure that your policy aligns precisely with your organisation's needs. Ambiguities or overly intricate clauses can lead to challenges during the claims process.

- ➤ **Exclusions and Limitations:** Thoroughly understand exclusions and limitations, particularly those related to nation-state attacks or third-party breaches, to prevent surprises when filing a claim.

- ➤ **Underinsurance:** Ensure your coverage limits are adequate to meet your potential financial exposure.

———∘○○-○○∘———

## Do's and Don'ts

➢ **Do:** Assess your risk profile. Conduct a comprehensive risk assessment to identify and prioritise potential threats.

➢ **Do:** Collaborate with insurers. Engage in open communication with insurers to comprehend policy terms, exclusions, and the claims process.

➢ **Do:** Compare policies from multiple insurers to find the best coverage and value.

➢ **Do:** Work closely with your IT and legal teams throughout the selection and claims process.

➢ **Don't:** Underestimate pre-existing conditions. Maintain transparency about your organisation's current cybersecurity posture to avoid coverage gaps.

➢ **Don't:** Set and Forget. Regularly review and update your cybersecurity measures and insurance coverage to adapt to evolving threats.

➢ **Don't:** Be afraid to negotiate policy terms and coverage limits.

Cyber insurance provides a proactive approach so that in the event of a cyberattack, you will have the necessary financial support to bounce back quickly and minimise the impact. This allows your small or

medium-sized enterprise or startup to stay focused on what truly matters: driving growth and fostering innovation.

❖   ❖   ❖   ❖

# BONUS #2 EFFECTIVE IMPLEMENTATION STEPS FOR DATA PROTECTION

To help you understand how your IT security team should successfully implement cybersecurity technologies, I am sharing these implementation steps with you. My goal is to give your team the confidence and know-how to tackle the challenges of cybersecurity in a way that makes sense for them.

## What is DLP?

Data Loss Prevention (DLP) encompasses software tools and processes aimed at safeguarding information in motion, at rest, and in use. DLP is implemented on endpoints, networks, and cloud platforms to ensure that users do not send private information via email or other means outside of the company's network. Its key functions include data/file discovery, classification based on business rules, monitoring, and protection.

DLP solutions are used across industries and sectors to reduce the risks associated with data breaches and ensure compliance with regulatory requirements. Organisations can deploy DLP solutions to monitor and control the movement of sensitive data across their networks, endpoints, and cloud systems. These solutions can identify and classify sensitive data, monitor data flows in real-time, enforce access controls, and apply encryption to prevent unauthorised access or leakage.

## Implementation Challenges

Many organisations struggle to implement a DLP solution due to network complexity, a distributed environment, a lack of centralised control over data/documents, and the absence of appropriate data classification mechanisms.

## Implementation Steps

> ➢ **Choose Your Deployment Areas:** Deploy DLP across email, web, and endpoints (including systems, USBs, and file transfers) to prevent data leakage across various channels.

> ➢ **Develop Data Policies:** Before DLP deployment, create data classification, handling, retention, and remediation policies tailored to your organisation's needs.

- ➢ **Apply Relevant Policies:** Utilise a variety of policy criteria, including:
  - Rule-Based/Regular Expressions
  - Database Fingerprinting
  - Exact File Matching
  - Partial Document Matching
  - Conceptual/Lexicon using Dictionaries and Rules
  - Statistical Analysis
  - Pre-built categories
- ➢ **Ensure policies are applied uniformly across the organisation.**
- ➢ **Procure a Comprehensive Solution:** Choose a DLP solution that caters to all users across endpoints, email, internet (proxy), and cloud-based DLP.
- ➢ **Employee Awareness:** Educate employees about the upcoming DLP implementation beforehand to ensure smooth adoption.
- ➢ **Implement Data Classification:** Deploy a data classification solution to categorise data based on sensitivity levels (e.g., internal, confidential, and public) and create corresponding DLP policies for actions such as audit, alert, and block.

➢ **Conduct Testing:** Test data classification and policy enforcement on a small scale with a few machines, emails, and content before moving to production.

➢ **Customise Policies:** Create separate group policies and integrate them with Active Directory (AD) to tailor policies based on user or department requirements.

➢ **Regular Review and Fine-tuning:** Conduct regular reviews, fine-tuning, and updates of DLP processes and policies to enhance effectiveness over time.

## DLP Solution Architecture

These examples offer a solid framework for deploying various technologies effectively. Remember, adaptability is key; tailor these principles to suit your specific needs and challenges. By harnessing similar approaches across different security solution deployments, you'll bolster your team's proficiency in navigating the ever-evolving landscape of technology implementations.

# BONUS #3 PRIVACY ASPECTS MAKING CYBERSECURITY MORE

Balancing innovation and user trust is crucial for sustainable growth, and implementing robust privacy practices is key. This chapter will explore key privacy principles to guide your business, while also aligning them with the General Data Protection Regulation (GDPR) and Organisation for Economic Cooperation and Development guidelines (OECD).

Here are some of the principles:

1.  Transparency and Accountability:

    - Be clear and concise about what data you collect, why you collect it, and how you use it.

    - Provide users with easily accessible information about their privacy rights and how to exercise them.

- Implement strong data governance practices and ensure accountability for data handling within your organisation.

2.  **Data Minimization:**

- Only collect and process data that is necessary for your legitimate business purposes.

- Avoid collecting sensitive data unless necessary and with explicit consent.

- Regularly review and delete data that are no longer needed.

3.  **Security and Integrity:**

- Implement appropriate technical and organisational measures to protect personal data from unauthorised access, disclosure, alteration, or destruction, as discussed in the earlier chapter.

- Regularly update your security measures to stay ahead of evolving threats.

- Report data breaches promptly and in accordance with relevant regulations.

4.  **User Choice and Control:**

- Give users meaningful control over their personal data, including the right to access, rectify, erase, and restrict processing.

- Respect user preferences regarding cookies, targeted advertising, and other data collection practices.

- Make it easy for users to exercise their privacy rights.

5. **Cross-Border Data Transfers:**

- Understand and comply with relevant data transfer regulations, such as the GDPR and relevant data transfer mechanisms.

- Implement appropriate safeguards to protect personal data transferred internationally.

6. **Privacy by Design:**

- Integrate privacy considerations into all aspects of your business operations, products, and services.

- Conduct privacy impact assessments for new projects and technologies.

- Seek expert advice when necessary to ensure compliance and best practices.

These privacy principles, incorporating both GDPR and OECD guidelines, provide a comprehensive framework for SMBs and start-ups to establish robust privacy practices and protect the personal data of their customers and employees. It's essential to tailor these principles to the specific needs and circumstances of

your business and seek legal advice if necessary to ensure compliance with applicable privacy laws and regulations. Remember, privacy is not just a compliance issue; it's a fundamental business value that fosters trust and strengthens your relationship with your customers.

# Conclusion

As we come to the end of this book, I hope you have gained a better understanding of cybersecurity and the challenges it presents. We have taken on the task of unravelling the complexities of this field, breaking them down into manageable pieces to help you protect your organisation's digital landscape.

I understand that breaking into the field of cybersecurity can feel like tackling a mountain of challenges. But remember, every big accomplishment starts with small steps. Focusing on the fundamentals and gradually increasing your defences, and helps you lay the groundwork for stronger and more resilient security.

With the knowledge you have gained here, combined with your determination and careful planning, I have no doubt that you will steer your organisation towards a safer digital future. Let us continue to protect our digital assets and pave the way for a world in which cybersecurity is both a priority and a requirement.

Join me on LinkedIn at

***https://www.linkedin.com/in/pgmahesh/***

Or scan the **QR code** below for access to valuable content aimed at safeguarding your organisation.

❖     ❖     ❖     ❖

# Abbreviations

- **BYOD-** Bring Your Own Device
- **CASB-** Cloud Access Security Broker
- **COBIT-** Control Objectives for Information and Related Technologies by ISACA
- **CSPM-** Cloud Security Posture Management
- **GDPR-** General Data Protection Rights
- **ISO-** International Organisation for Standardisation
- **NIST-** National Institute of Standards and Technology
- **OECD-** Organisation for Economic Co-Operation and Development
- **SaaS-** Software as a Service
- **SOC Report-** Service Organisation Control Report
- **SMB-** Small and Medium Business

# REFERENCES


1. https://nvlpubs.nist.gov/nistpubs/CSWP/NIST.CSWP.29.pdf

2. https://www.lockheedmartin.com/en-us/capabilities/cyber/cyber-kill-chain.html

3. https://csrc.nist.gov/pubs/sp/800/61/r2/final

4. https://gdpr-info.eu

5. https://www.dataprotection.ie/en/organisations/know-your-obligations/data-protection-impact-assessments

6. https://www.oecd.org/sti/ieconomy/oecd_privacy_framework.pdf

7. https://www.kaseya.com/press-release/kaseya-responds-swiftly-to-sophisticated-cyberattack-mitigating-global-disruption-to-customers/

8. https://www.nytimes.com/2021/05/13/us/politics/biden-colonial-pipeline-ransomware.html

9. https://www.sans.org/blog/what-you-need-to-know-about-the-solarwinds-supply-chain-attack/

10. https://www.techtarget.com/searchsecurity/definition/WannaCry-ransomware

11. https://archive.epic.org/privacy/data-breach/equifax/

12. https://www.cisa.gov/news-events/
alerts/2017/07/01/petya-ransomware

13. https://www.bbc.com/news/technology-42075306
(Uber data breach)

14. https://www.theguardian.com/technology/2016/
oct/26/ddos-attack-dyn-mirai-botnet

15. https://news.marriott.com/news/2018/11/30/
marriott-announces-starwood-guest-reservation-
database-security-incident

16. https://www.cshub.com/attacks/articles/
incident-of-the-week-garmin-pays-10-million-
to-ransomware-hackers-who-rendered-systems-
useless

# Praise for the Book

"Cyber Resilience for Entrepreneurs" by Mahesh, simplifies complex concepts into manageable steps. The real-life examples and practical advice make it easy to absorb. The book thoroughly covers everything from identifying threats to implementing modern solutions, all in an easy-to-understand format.

**-Sesha Phani Babu Turimella,**

Industry Principal, Infosys Limited, India

***

A comprehensive guide that demystifies complex cyber security concepts with its lucid explanation. The author's experience and expertise make this book an invaluable resource for both for beginners and experienced professionals.

**-Shibu P S,**

Cybersecurity Leader, Large Financial Organisation, Middle East

***

I found "Cyber Resilience for Entrepreneurs" by Mahesh not only helps you understand the importance of Cybersecurity but also provides clear steps to take action to protect business amid digital security challenges, especially protecting client data.

**-Dr. Meghana Dikshit,**

Entrepreneur, Brain Rewiring Expert, TedX Speaker, De Mantraa, India

***

As a small business owner, cybersecurity always seemed like a BIG DEAL. However, 'Cyber Resilience for Entrepreneurs' breaks it down into manageable steps. The real-life examples and advice made everything easy to take in. Highly recommended!

**-Anil Kumar Bathini,**

Principal Consultant, Infosys Limited, India

***

Cybersecurity is a topic that often looks difficult, especially for SMBs. This book, though, makes it incredibly accessible. Such a valuable resource for any business owner!

**-Smrithi R Ambatt,**

Assistant Professor, Bangalore Technological Institute, India

***

Honestly, I have been looking for a practical guide to cybersecurity for my startup, and this book from Mahesh delivered exactly what I needed. It is filled with actionable strategies that I could implement right away. A must-read for any entrepreneur serious about protecting their digital assets.

### -Praveen Siinghhal,

Lawyer and CEO at Edvisars Consultancy Services, India

***

In this digital era, it is vital to protect Digital Assets whilst ensuring cybersecurity is an enabler for businesses and organizations. Mahesh had put his practical experience with "Cyber Resilience for Entrepreneurs" and made it easy to understand, especially for startups and entrepreneurs, for whom I strongly suggest this book with an aim to safeguard their Digital assets.

### -Praveen Kumar MOTUPALLI,

Cybersecurity Leader, Harvard MLE, Bangalore, India

———○○○○○○———

"Cyber Resilience for Entrepreneurs" is a vital guide for SMBs and startups, simplifying cybersecurity with practical advice and real-life examples. Covering key topics from threat understanding to leveraging modern technology, it empowers your business to mitigate risks and achieve digital success.

### -Ashok Kumar Ratnagiri,

AVP – Senior Director & Head Information Security, EdgeVerve, India

"Cyber Resilience for Entrepreneurs" is a must-have for SMBs and startups, offering clear guidance on protecting digital assets. With expert insights and real-life examples, it covers key topics like threat identification, security awareness, and compliance. This book provides essential strategies for managing cyber risks and achieving digital success.

### -Dr. J. Balasubramanian,

Professor and HOD, Info Institute of Engineering, India

***